A POCKET BOOK OF SPIRITUAL POEMS

A Pocket Book of Spiritual Poems

Edited by Rumer Godden
1993–1995 – and a lifetime

Hodder & Stoughton
LONDON SYDNEY AUCKLAND

British Library Cataloguing in Publication Data
A record for this book is available from the British Library

ISBN 0 340 643056

Typeset by Hewer Text Composition Services, Edinburgh
Printed and bound in Great Britain by
Mackays of Chatham PLC, Chatham, Kent

Hodder and Stoughton Ltd
A Division of Hodder Headline PLC
338 Euston Road
London NW1 3BH

He who binds to himself a joy
Does the wingèd life destroy;
But he who kisses the joy as it flies
Lives in Eternity's sunrise

'Eternity', WILLIAM BLAKE

Contents

FOREWORD

*T*his does not make any claim to be representative of spiritual poetry; it is simply a book of poems that, to me, truly belong to this realm and that I have loved and lived with in my long years.

Some are so well known they may seem almost too familiar but it is love that has made them so; others may be new to the reader – I am discovering new ones all the time. Some are minor; others so majestically major that they have to be read, re-read, pondered on and said over and over again before one can fathom their full richness.

It is based on the Christian year, beginning and ending with Advent, but there are poems from many creeds because, as that most lovable of Hindu gods Krishna says, 'All paths men take on all sides lead to Me.'

Nor is this book to be read through – one would soon have indigestion. It is meant to be dipped into, kept in a pocket or handbag, by a bedside. I can only hope the poems will give to other people the help, calm and joy they have brought to me.

R. G.

Advent

*A*dvent, of course, means 'coming' yet it is far more portentous than that, portentous even to the supernatural, particularly the Christian Advent, which was to change the world and was, above all, the fulfilment of a promise.

God's promises are firm – 'Let there be light, and there was light'[1] – even though it might have taken a milliard years. His sense of time is not ours. Sometimes, too, a promise comes to pass in such an extraordinary way that it is difficult for us to understand, let alone believe, but did He not warn us: 'My thoughts are not your thoughts, neither are your ways my ways'?[2]

Often, too, God makes His promises through His prophets; Isaiah, centuries before Christ was born, wrote in his Book, 'Behold, a virgin shall conceive, and bear a son, and shall call his name Immanuel,'[3] and again, 'For unto us a child is born, unto us a son is given ... and his name shall be called Wonderful, Counsellor, The Mighty God ... The Prince of Peace'.[4] Isaiah seems to have written almost a fifth gospel; he even foretells Christ's Passion and Crucifixion, and in what vivid words! More than seven hundred years later – not even a day in God's time – that promise too was fulfilled.

1 Genesis 1:3 (King James Bible).
2 Isaiah 55:8 (King James Bible).
3 Isaiah 7:14 (King James Bible).
4 Isaiah 9:6 (King James Bible).

The Starlight Night

Look at the stars! look, look up at the skies!
O look at all the fire-folk sitting in the air!
The bright boroughs, the circle-citadels
there!
Down in dim woods the diamond delves! the
elves'-eyes!
The grey lawns cold where gold, where
quickgold lies!
Wind-beat whitebeam! airy abeles set on a
flare!
Flake-doves sent floating forth at a
farmyard scare! –
Ah well! it is all a purchase, all is a prize.

Buy then! bid then! – What? – Prayer,
patience, alms, vows.
Look, look . . .

Gerard Manley Hopkins

$\mathcal{S}$ONNET

Bright star, would I were stedfast as thou art –
   Not in lone splendour hung aloft the night
And watching, with eternal lids apart,
   Like nature's patient, sleepless Eremite,
The moving waters at their priestlike task
   Of pure ablution round earth's human
      shores,
Or gazing on the new soft-fallen mask
   Of snow upon the mountains and the
      moors –
No – yet still stedfast, still unchangeable . . .

                    John Keats

The heavens declare the glory of God; and the firmament sheweth his handywork.

Day unto day uttereth speech, and night unto night sheweth knowledge.

There is no speech nor language, where their voice is not heard.

Their line is gone out through all the earth, and their words to the end of the world. In them hath he set a tabernacle for the sun.

Which is as a bridegroom coming out of his chamber, and rejoiceth as a strong man to run a race.

His going forth is from the end of the heaven, and his circuit under the ends of it: and there is nothing hid from the heat thereof.

The law of the Lord is perfect, converting the soul: the testimony of the Lord is sure, making wise the simple.

The statutes of the Lord are right, rejoicing the heart: the commandment of the Lord is pure, enlightening the eyes.

The fear of the Lord is clean, enduring for ever: the judgments of the Lord are true and righteous altogether.

More to be desired are they than gold, yea, than much fine gold: sweeter also than honey and the honeycomb.

Moreover by them is thy servant warned: and in keeping of them there is great reward.

(King James Bible)

Batter My Heart, Three-Person'd God

Batter my heart, three-person'd God; for, you
As yet but knocke, breathe, shine, and seeke to
   mend;
That I may rise, and stand, o'erthrow mee . . .
   and bend
Your force, to breake, blowe, burn and make
   me new.
I, like an usurpt towne, to'another due,
Labour to'admit you, but Oh, to no end,
Reason your viceroy in mee, mee should
   defend,
But is captiv'd, and proves weake or untrue.
Yet dearly'I love you,'and would be loved
   faine,
But am betroth'd unto your enemie:
Divorce mee, 'untie, or breake that knot againe,
Take mee to you, imprison mee, for I
Except you'enthrall mee, never shall be free,
Nor ever chast, except you ravish mee.

John Donne

GOD BE IN MY HEAD

God be in my head
And in my understanding;

God be in mine eyes
And in my looking;

God be in my mouth
And in my speaking;

God be in my heart
And in my thinking;

God be at my end
And in my departing.

Anon.

From The Flower

Who would have thought my shrivell'd heart
Could have recovered greenness? It was gone
  Quite underground; as flowers depart
To feed their mother-root, when they have
  blown,
          Where they together
          All the hard weather,
Dead to the world, keep house unknown.

These are Thy wonders, Lord of power,
Killing and quickening, bringing down to Hell
And up to Heaven in an hour;
Making a chiming of a passing bell.
          We say amiss,
          This or that is;
Thy word is all, if we could spell.

George Herbert

The Call

Come, my Way, my Truth, my Life!
Such a Way as gives us breath:
Such a Truth as ends all strife:
Such a Life as killeth Death.

Come, my Light, my Feast, my Strength!
Such a light as shows a feast:
Such a Feast as mends in length:
Such a Strength as makes his guest.

Come, my Joy, my Love, my Heart!
Such a Joy as none can move:
Such a Love as none can part:
Such a Heart as joys in love.

George Herbert

CHRISTMAS

The bells of waiting Advent ring,
  The Tortoise stove is lit again
And lamp-oil light across the night
  Has caught the streaks of winter rain
In many a stained-glass window sheen
From Crimson Lake to Hooker's Green.

The holly in the windy hedge
  And round the Manor House the yew
Will soon be stripped to deck the ledge,
  The altar, font and arch and pew,
So that the villagers can say
'The church looks nice' on Christmas Day.

Provincial public houses blaze
  And Corporation tramcars clang,
On lighted tenements I gaze
  Where paper decorations hang,
And bunting in the red Town Hall
Says 'Merry Christmas to you all'.

And London shops on Christmas Eve
  Are strung with silver bells and flowers
As hurrying clerks the City leave
  To pigeon-haunted classic towers,
And marbled clouds go scudding by
The many-steepled London sky.

And girls in slacks remember Dad,
    And oafish louts remember Mum,
And sleepless children's hearts are glad,
    And Christmas-morning bells say 'Come!'
Even to shining ones who dwell
Safe in the Dorchester Hotel.

And is it true? And is it true,
    This most tremendous tale of all,
Seen in a stained-glass window's hue,
    A Baby in an ox's stall?
The Maker of the stars and sea
Become a Child on earth for me?

And is it true? For if it is,
    No loving fingers tying strings
Around those tissued fripperies,
    The sweet and silly Christmas things,
Bath salts and inexpensive scent
And hideous tie so kindly meant,

No love that in a family dwells,
    No carolling in frosty air,
Nor all the steeple-shaking bells
    Can with this single Truth compare –
That God was Man in Palestine
And lives today in Bread and Wine.

John Betjeman

FROM HAMLET, ACT I, SC. I

Some say that ever 'gainst that season comes
Wherein our Saviour's birth is celebrated,
The bird of dawning singeth all night long;
And then, they say, no spirit can walk abroad;
The nights are wholesome; then no planets strike,
No fairy takes, nor witch hath power to charm,
So hallow'd and so gracious is the time.

William Shakespeare

$\mathcal{T}$HE $\mathcal{O}$XEN

Christmas Eve, and twelve of the clock.
   'Now they are all on their knees,'
An elder said as we sat in a flock
   By the embers in hearthside ease.

We pictured the meek mild creatures where
   They dwelt in their strawy pen,
Nor did it occur to one of us there
   To doubt they were kneeling then.

So fair a fancy few would weave
   In these years! Yet, I feel,
If someone said on Christmas Eve,
   'Come; see the oxen kneel

In the lonely barton by yonder coomb
   Our childhood used to know,'
I should go with him in the gloom,
   Hoping it might be so.

Thomas Hardy

CHRISTMAS

Though never forgetting the awe and wonder of the miracle for which they had been singled out, the great strength of Mary and Joseph is the way they accepted it; nothing could have been more simple, humble and down to earth.

Joseph, as with the rest of his world, had, by edict, to go to his home town of Bethlehem to be taxed. It cannot have been a convenient time for Mary to travel, but it seems never to have crossed his mind not to take her with him – had he not been divinely appointed to look after her? When, at the journey's end, there was no room for them at the inn, instead of lamenting or pleading they quietly accepted – one can guess thankfully – the offer of the stable.

There is a strong belief that St Luke wrote his Gospel from Mary's own telling of it to him. How else could he have known? None of the other gospels gives any account of Jesus's actual birth. St Luke was a doctor and tells it in the plainest way: 'she brought forth her firstborn son, and wrapped him in swaddling clothes, and laid him in a manger.'[1]

Many devout women say, 'I'm glad she knew the pains of labour and so can feel with us,' but there is a very old saying – and belief – that Jesus left his mother like a sun-ray coming through a pane of glass without breaking it; perhaps that explains the Church's 'Blessed Mary, ever a virgin'.[2]

1 Luke 2:7 (King James Bible).

2 This was told to me by that learned nun, Dame Felicitas Corrigan, OSB, of Stanbrook Abbey.

A Woman at Christmas

Let me kindle Christmas,
let me find the meaning,
the being
in this doing and coming and going,
life flowing
but broken into bright pieces for the festival.
Let me make my house hospitable.
Mary, mother, is on her way to Bethlehem;
Is Mary, Martha's sister, listening?

For neighbours, family and friends,
the breath of life in Martha's hands
brings beauty: fires, white beds, clean rooms;
it shines in soapsuds, ovens, brooms,
in still room,
store-room,
larder,
cellar,
in bread and wine, plum puddings, turkey meat.
There are angel wings on Martha's tired feet
but gold and frankincense and myrrh,
symbols through the centuries, to her
are tinsel, crackers, spangles,
red candles
on the Christmas tree. Peace on earth and
  mercy mild?

The inn is crowded with Christmas. Is there
    still no room for the Child?
No quiet to hear the quiet, the new heart
    beating, quickening, waking?
Yes, Mary, Martha's sister, is waiting.

The snow falls from a quiet sky
and now the house is quiet, the children lie
sleeping; the nativity
crib is lit; candles shine on white
banisters and the holly's green and red,
and Mary, Martha's sister, keeps
vigil while weary Martha sleeps.
From the four corners of the earth the rough
    ways meet in the centre of the Cross
where Christ incarnate is born in a crib of
    sawdust, clay and moss.

Then with Martha I need Mary,
and with Mary I need Martha,
to kindle Christmas. Let the lit candle be
homely light, holy light,
to bless our house and bless its hospitality.

Rumer Godden

He Came All So Still

... He came all so still
Where his mother was,
As dew in April
That falleth on the grass.

He came all so still
To his mother's bower,
As dew in April
That falleth on the flower.

He came all so still
Where his mother lay,
As dew in April
That falleth on the spray.

Mother and maiden
Was never none but she;
Well may such a lady
Godes mother be.

Anon.

THE FOURTH SHEPHERD

AND THIS SHALL BE A SIGN UNTO YOU; YE
SHALL FIND THE BABE WRAPPED IN
SWADDLING CLOTHES, LYING IN A
MANGER (LUKE 2:12)

The four strange men knelt down to see
   The Boy that sleeping lay
And three were full of ecstasy,
   But one said, softly: 'Nay.'
And he that so denied went out
   Into the starry calm,
For, somewhere in the dark, he thought
   He heard a bleating lamb.
With heartstrings tight with pity, he
   Forgot the child within,
And Mary and his comrades three,
   And counted it no sin.
Back all the weary way he trod,
   And paused not once for sleep;
   That child may be the Son of God,
   But I must guard my sheep!'

A. M. Davidson

I love this byre. Shadows are kindly here.
The light is flecked with travelling stars of
    dust.
So quiet it seems after the inn-clamour,
Scraping of fiddles and the stamping feet.
Only the cows, each in her patient box,
Turn their slow eyes, as we and the sunlight
    enter,
Their slowly rhythmic mouths.
         . . . "That is the stall,
Carpenter. You see it's too far gone
For patching or repatching. My husband
    made it,
And he's been gone these dozen years and
    more . . ."
. . . That board there
Baring its knot-hole like a missing jig-saw —
I remember another hand along its rim.
No, not my husband's, and why I should
    remember
I cannot say. It was a night in winter.
Our house was full, tight-packed as salted
    herrings —
So full, they said, we had to hold our
    breaths

To close the door and shut the night-air
  out!
And then two travellers came. They stood
  outside
Across the threshold, half in the ring of
  light
And half beyond it. I would have let them in
Despite the crowding – the woman was past
  her time –
But I'd no mind to argue with my
  husband.
The flagon in my hand and half the inn
Still clamouring for wine. But when trade
  slackened,
And all our guests had sung themselves to
  bed
Or told the floor their troubles, I came out
  here
Where he had lodged them. The man was
  standing
As you are now, his hand smoothing that
  board –
He was a carpenter, I heard them say.
She rested on the straw, and on her arm
A child was lying. None of your creased-faced
  brats
Squalling their lungs out. Just lying there
As calm as a new-dropped calf – his eyes
  wide open

And gazing round as if the world he saw
In the chaff-strewn light of the stable lantern
Was something beautiful and new and
strange.

Clive Sansom

ℒucy's ℂarol

When the Baby borned
Joseph said to Mary,
'What am I going to do about
This little-born Jesus Baby Christ?
I never knew it was going to be like this,
With all these angels and kings
And shepherds and stars and things;
It's got me worried, I can tell you,
On Christmas Day in the morning.'

Mary said to Joseph,
'Not to worry, my darling,
Dear old darling Joseph;
Everything's going to be all right,
Because the Angel told me not to fear;
So just hold up the lamp,
So I can see the dear funny sweet little face
Of my darling little-born Jesus Baby Christ.'

Joseph said to Mary,
'Behold the handyman of the Lord!'

Happy Christmas, happy Christmas!
Christ is born today.

**(Lucy was five years old when she
composed it; her mother wrote it down
exactly as it came)**

LITTLE TREE

little tree
little silent Christmas tree
you are so little
you are more like a flower

who found you in the green forest
and were you very sorry to come away?
see   i will comfort you
because you smell so sweetly

i will kiss your cool bark
and hug you safe and tight
just as your mother would,
only don't be afraid

look   the spangles
that sleep all the year in a dark box
dreaming of being taken out and allowed to shine,
the balls the chains red and gold the fluffy threads,

put up your little arms
and i'll give them all to you to hold
every finger shall have its ring
and there won't be a single place dark or unhappy

then when you're quite dressed
you'll stand in the window for everyone to see

and how they'll stare!
oh but you'll be very proud
and my little sister and i will take hands
and looking up at our beautiful tree
we'll dance and sing
'Noel Noel'

E. E. Cummings

$\mathcal{E}$DDI'S $\mathcal{S}$ERVICE

WHERE TWO OR THREE ARE GATHERED
TOGETHER IN MY NAME, THERE AM I IN
THE MIDST OF THEM (MATTHEW 18:20)

Eddi, priest of St Wilfrid
In the chapel at Manhood End,
Ordered a midnight Service
For such as cared to attend.

But the Saxons were keeping Christmas,
And the night was stormy as well.
Nobody came to service,
Though Eddi rang the bell.

'Wicked weather for walking,'
Said Eddi of Manhood End.
'But I must go on with the service
For such as care to attend.'

The altar candles were lighted
An old marsh-donkey came,
Bold as a guest invited,
And stared at the guttering flame.

The storm beat on at the windows,
The water splashed on the floor,
And a wet, yoke-weary bullock
Pushed in through the open door.

'How do I know what is greatest?
How do I know what is least?
That is my Father's business,'
Said Eddi, Wilfrid's priest.

'But – three are gathered together –
Listen to me and attend.
I bring good news, my brethren!'
Said Eddi of Manhood End.

And he told the ox of a manger
And a stall in Bethlehem,
And he spoke to the ass of a rider
That rode to Jerusalem.

They steamed and dripped in the chancel,
They listened and never stirred
While, just as though they were bishops,
Eddi preached to them the Word.

Till the gale blew off on the marshes
And the windows showed the day,
And the ox and the ass together
Wheeled and clattered away.

And when the Saxons mocked him,
Said Eddi of Manhood End,
'I dare not shut the chapel
On such as care to attend.'

Rudyard Kipling

ANNUNCIATION

The world seems to prefer to think of Mary as a simple village girl, but if we study the first chapter of Luke, it is clear she must have been far more than that. Her cousin, Elizabeth, was married to Zacharias, the High Priest, and though Elizabeth was older, she was obviously close to Mary – it was to Elizabeth that she fled when it had become manifest that all that the angel had told her was becoming true. Through Zacharias, Mary would have known the Scriptures – prophecies, miracles, angels were not strange words to her – but when a live Gabriel greeted her with a salutation: 'Hail thou that are highly favoured, the Lord is with thee: blessed art thou among women' – she and no one else – it was no wonder that she was 'troubled at his saying and cast in her mind what manner of salutation this should be'.[1]

She has, too, always been held up as an example of perfect obedience, as if she had said, '*Fiat*' ('let it be done'), as soon as Gabriel had ended his message, but she was not so obedient as Joseph, who was to do as he was told without a cavil; in all the Bible, Joseph does not speak a word – he acts. Mary asked one question, a sensible and natural one for a young girl, though even then she was not doubting. She did not say, 'This cannot be because I know not a man,' but 'How shall this be . . . ?' and listened while Gabriel told her the whole, ending, '. . . with God nothing shall be impossible.'

It is strange that Joseph is so often shown as an old, grey-headed man – perhaps because old men are supposed to be wiser and without such a strong sexual urge, but that detracts from his courage, selflessness and strength. He must have needed all a young man's energy and ardour to do what he did; for instance, at the command in the middle of the night, 'Arise, and take the young child and his mother, and flee into Egypt,'[2] he got them up and went at once.

Of Mary's father and mother there is no mention in the Gospels but, in the belief that has grown in Christendom, they are called Joachim and Anne, and St Anne is often shown in paintings with Mary, Jesus and the little John the Baptist, giving a family feeling. St Anne, too, has touchingly become the patron saint of cupboard makers because she once held Mary in the secret cupboard of her womb.

1 Luke; 28–9 (King James Bible).
2 Matthew 2:13 (King James Bible).

MARY OF NAZARETH

This is the miracle
that virginity given of God
can only be broken by man –
now I am alone among my companions
for that I stand tall and narrow
my robe straight and neat about my cool
   round knees
my girdle clasped as usual by my own fingers

how can this thing be in my young spring
when anemones spill over the rocky hill
incarnadine
is it the nature of girls to bewail their virginity
whether or no –
for me all I know
since the shining wings overshadowed me
the light of his countenance stilled my fear
is the birth of song in my soul

O my beloved is the young roe
he leaps upon the mountains of Bether
he feeds among the lilies
my musings are become his pastures my eyes
   are upon him
with clear shining after rain

Mary Casey

Concerning The Divine Word

With the divinest Word, the Virgin,
Made pregnant, comes walking
Down the road, if you'll grant her
A room in your abode.

St John of the Cross (Tr. Roy Campbell)

From The Morning Watch

O Joys! Infinite sweetness! with what flowers,
And shoots of glory, my soul breaks, and buds!
　　　All the long hours
　　　Of night, and rest,
　　　Through the still shrouds
　　　Of sleep, and clouds,
　　His dew fell on my breast;
　　　O, how it bloods,
And spirits all my earth! hark! in what rings,
And hymning circulations the quick world
　　　Awakes, and sings;
　　　The rising winds
　　　And falling springs,
　　　Birds, beasts, all things
　　Adore him in their kinds.
　　　Thus all is hurled
In sacred hymns and order, the greater chime
And symphony of nature. Prayer is
　　　The world in tune,
　　　A spirit-voice,
　　　And vocal joys
　　Whose echo's heaven's bliss.
　　　O, let me climb,
When I lie down. The pious soul by night

Is like a clouded star, whose beams though said
               To shed their light
               Under some cloud,
               Yet are above,
               And shine and move
             Beyond that misty shroud.
               So in my bed,
That curtained grave, though sleep, like ashes,
    hide
My lamp, and life, both shall in thee abide.

                              Henry Vaughan

$\int$ PRING

Nothing is so beautiful as spring –
    When weeds, in wheels, shoot long and
       lovely and lush;
    Thrush's eggs look little low heavens, and
       thrush
Through the echoing timber does so rinse and
    wring
The ear, it strikes like lightnings to hear him sing;
    The glassy peartree leaves and blooms, they
       brush
    The descending blue; that blue is all in a rush
With richness; the racing lambs too have fair
    their fling.

What is all this juice and all this joy?
    A strain of the earth's sweet being in the
       beginning
           In Eden garden. – Have, get, before
           it cloy,
    Before it cloud, Christ, lord, and sour with
       sinning,
Innocent mind and Mayday in girl and boy,
Most, O maid's child, thy choice and worthy
    the winning.

Gerard Manley Hopkins

From Fern Hill

AND THE CHILD GREW, AND WAXED
STRONG IN SPIRIT (LUKE 2:40)

Now as I was young and easy under the apple
  boughs
About the lilting house and happy as the grass
  was green,
     The night above the dingle starry,
      Time let me hail and climb
     Golden in the heydays of his eyes,
And honoured among wagons I was prince of
  the apple towns
And once below a time I lordly had the trees
  and leaves
        Trail with daisies and barley
      Down the rivers of the windfall light.

And as I was green and carefree, famous
  among the barns
About the happy yard and singing as the farm
  was home,
     In the sun that is young once only,
      Time let me play and be
     Golden in the mercy of his means,
And green and golden I was huntsman and
  herdsman, the calves

Sang to my horn, the foxes on the hills barked
   clear and cold,
            And the sabbath rang slowly
   In the pebbles of the holy streams.

Dylan Thomas

Timothy Winters

Timothy Winters comes to school
With eyes as wide as a football pool,
Ears like bombs and teeth like splinters:
A blitz of a boy is Timothy Winters.

His belly is white, his neck is dark,
And his hair is an exclamation mark,
His clothes are enough to scare a crow
And through his britches the blue winds blow.

When teacher talks he won't hear a word
And he shoots down dead the arithmetic-bird,
He licks the patterns off his plate
And he's not even heard of the Welfare State.

Timothy Winters has bloody feet
And he lives in a house on Suez Street,
He sleeps in a sack on the kitchen floor
And they say there aren't boys like him any
    more.

Old Man Winters likes his beer
And his missus ran off with a bombadier,
Grandma sits in the grate with a gin
And Timothy's dosed with an aspirin.

The Welfare Worker lies awake
But the law's as tricky as a ten-foot snake,
So Timothy Winters drinks his cup
And slowly goes on growing up.

At Morning Prayers the Master helves*
For children less fortunate than ourselves,
And the loudest response in the room is when
Timothy Winters roars 'Amen!'

So come one angel, come on ten:
Timothy Winters says 'Amen
Amen amen amen amen.'
Timothy Winters, Lord.
                    Amen.

Charles Causley

*By 'helves' the poet means the Headmaster goes on and on.

Mistral to the Children
(A LOS NIÑOS)

Many years from now, when I am a little heap of silenced dust, play with me, with the earth of my heart and my bones. If a mason were to gather me up, he would make me into a brick, and I should remain locked forever into a wall; and I hate quiet crevices. If they made me into a brick for a prison, I should redden with shame to have to hear the men sob; and if I became a brick in a schoolhouse, it would pain me, too, not to be able to sing with you in the mornings.

Rather, I should like to be the dust you play with along the country roads. Squeeze me: I shall have been yours; crumble me, for having been the one who made you; trample upon me, for not having given you all truth and all beauty. Or simply sing and run upon me, that I may kiss your dear soles.

Recite a pretty verse when you have me in your hands, and I will throb with joy between your fingers. I will stand up tall to watch you, seeking among you the eyes, the hair of those I taught.

And when you shape me into some figure, keep shattering it, as you in your tenderness and sorrow shattered me.

Anon. (tr. Kate Flores)

LENT

*W*hy does anyone keep Lent? The answer is quite simple: for the joy it brings. Joy? That time of come-uppance penance? What a paradox! But paradoxes can be true in unexpected depth.[1] The Oxford Dictionary, that reliable and exact source, gives us the clue: Lent is 'a surrender of something valued, for the sake of something having a higher and more pressing claim', which, of course, entails sacrifice: in Lent, sacrifice of our very selves.

All the great religions of the world follow the same ideal. A Hindu wife will fast one set day a week, not for herself but for the well-being of her husband because when he has to work hard he doesn't have time for *puja* (prayer). It is ironic that if she works too, as she frequently does these days, she still often keeps her 'day'. Islam has the month of Ramadan when, from sunrise to sunset, the faithful Muslim must not eat or drink – not even a sip of water, which can be cruel if Ramadan falls in hot weather. We Christians have the forty days of Lent as a time for penitence and fasting, from which, if we are honest, most of us, except the truly ardent, shrink.

'Fasting' is a dramatic word with a tincture of the fanatical, even of morbidity, though not when it is done for the purpose of health or slimming, which everyone can understand and admire; there has never been an age when people were so preoccupied – it can be *obsessed* – by their bodies.

A body has a brain, a heart, and a mind – adequate, one might say, yet it needs something more; a baby in the womb normally has the potentiality of all three, but it cannot begin to use them until it 'quickens', just as, in the biblical allegory of Adam and Eve, when God made the first man, Adam, of dust – which has its own significance. Adam could not move until God breathed into him, giving him the breath of life – his spirit, and so it is with all of us. But the spirit, just as much as the body, needs curbing, which is why wisdom provides these times of self-denial.

Lent has a difference in that it is for not only 'giving up' but 'giving out', not only abnegation but affirmation, acting instead of comfortably drifting. Perhaps it makes us pray more, read more, think more deeply, do an unwelcome duty which we have tried to dodge, make something – in a minor way, create.

Ramadan ends with the first sight of the new moon, the Id moon, and one of the most joyous festivals in the world.[2] 'But I couldn't enjoy it so much,' says the young Muslim Aziz, 'if I hadn't kept the fast. Now I can respect myself.'

There is, at the end, satisfaction; we have achieved at least a measure of self-control, and it is that which brings joy – we all know how much more we value things if we have to go without them. And, beyond satisfaction, there comes a sense of purification, as long as we don't spoil it.

Jesus was extraordinarily sensible about this, and gave us clear warnings about fasting: first, keep quiet about it (unlike the health-seekers for whom their diets and rules are an endless topic): 'When you fast do not put on a gloomy look as the hypocrites do: they pull long faces to let men know they are fasting. I tell you solemnly, they have had their reward. But when you fast, put oil on your head and wash your face, so that no one will know you are fasting except your Father who sees all that is done in secret . . . in secret will reward you.'[3]

And do not be too rigid: 'Then came to him the disciples of John the Baptist, saying, "Why do we and the Pharisees fast oft, but thy disciples fast not?" And Jesus said, "Can the children of the bridechamber mourn, as long as the bridegroom is with them?" '[4]

We are all likely, in Lent, to meet 'bridegroom occasions', when it would be churlish – more: wrong – to refuse to join in the eating and drinking.

With every faith the chief joy is that these days and weeks set apart bring us closer to our God, no matter what our creed; for Christians, to God's son, Jesus Christ, in that our sacrifice, no matter how small, allows us an infinitesimal share in his sufferings and the marvel of the joy of Easter:

> As perchance, Carvers do not faces make,
> But that away, which hid them here, do take;
> Let Crosses, soe, take what hid Christ in thee,
> And be his image, or not his, but hee . . .[5]

1 For instance, many Christians dislike St Paul because he is so strict, yet he wrote the greatest and wisest paean to love ever known.

2 See poem on p. 52.

3 Matthew 6:16–18 (Jerusalem Bible).

4 ibid., 9:14–15 (King James Bible).

5 *From* 'The Crosse' by John Donne.

To Keep a True Lent

CHRISTIANS HAVE THE FORTY DAYS OF
LENT AND PENANCE

Is this a Fast, to keep
The larder lean?
  And clean
From fat of veals and sheep?

Is it to quit the dish
Of flesh, yet still
  To fill
The platter high with fish?

Is it to fast an hour,
Or ragg'd to go,
  Or show
A down-cast look and sour?

No: 'tis a Fast to dole
Thy sheaf of wheat
  And meat
Unto the hungry soul.

It is to fast from strife
And old debate,
  And hate;
To circumcise thy life.

To show a heart grief-rent;
To starve thy sin,
   Not bin;
And that's to keep thy Lent.

Robert Herrick

From Bishop Blougram's Apology

No, when the fight begins within himself,
A man's worth something. God stoops o'er his
   head,
Satan looks up between his feet – both tug –
He's left himself, i' the middle: the soul wakes
And grows. Prolong that battle through his life!

Robert Browning

A Hymn to God the Father

Wilt thou forgive that sinne where I begunne,
  Which was my sin, though it were done
    before?
Wilt though forgive that sinne; through which
  I runne,
    And do run still: though still I do deplore?
      When thou hast done, thou hast not
      done,
            For, I have more.

Wilt thou forgive that sinne which I have
  wonne
    Others to sinne? and, made my sinne their
    doore?
Wilt thou forgive that sinne which I did
  shunne
    A yeare, or two: but wallowed in, a score?
      When thou hast done, thou hast not
      done,
            For I have more.

I have a sinne of feare, that when I have
  spunne
    My last thred, I shall perish on the shore;
But sweare by thy selfe, that at my death thy
  sonne

Shall shine as he shines now, and
  heretofore;
And having done that, Thou hast done,
  I feare no more.

John Donne

I CAME OUT ALONE ON MY WAY TO MY TRYST

I came out alone on my way to my tryst. But
   who is this that follows me in the silent dark?
   I move aside to avoid this presence but I
     escape him not.
   He makes the dust rise from the earth with
     his swagger; he adds his loud voice to
     every word that I utter.
   He is my own little self, my lord, he knows
     no shame; but
I am ashamed to come to thy door in his
   company.

Rabindranath Tagore

$\mathscr{L}$OVE

Love bade me welcome: yet my soul drew back,
      Guiltie of dust and sinne.
But quick-ey'd Love, observing me grow slack
      From my first entrance in,
Drew nearer to me, sweetly questioning,
      If I lack'd any thing.

A guest, I answer'd, worthy to be here:
      Love said, You shall be he.
I the unkinde, ungratefull? Ah my deare,
      I cannot look on thee.
Love took my hand and smiling did reply,
      Who made the eyes but I?

Truth Lord, but I have marr'd them: let my
   shame
      Go where it doth deserve.
And know you not, sayes Love, who bore the
   blame?
      My deare, then I will serve.
You must sit down, sayes Love, and taste my
   meat:
      So I did sit and eat.

George Herbert

Hope Is the Thing with Feathers

Hope is the thing with feathers
That perches in the soul,
And sings the tune without the words
And never stops at all,

And sweetest in the gale is heard;
And sore must be the storm
That could abash the little bird
That kept so many warm.

I've heard it in the chillest land,
And on the strangest sea;
Yet, never, in extremity,
It asked a crumb of me.

Emily Dickinson

Little Id Moon

Tahira, Fahmeeda,
Shameen Khatoon,
All dance together for
The little Id moon.

Dance in a circle
In the lit room,
Dance all together for
The little Id moon.

This way
That way
Three in a line,
Three feet
Beating
All in time.

Noodles this evening,
Pulao at noon,
Sweet yellow rice
For you, little moon.

Bibiji* fasted
A whole month long;
Now it's all over
Let's sing a song!

'O, thread of silver,
Night's precious boon
Rising within us,
Little Id moon!'

Farida Bedi

*Bibiji: grandmother

*E*ASTER

I got me flowers to straw thy way;
I got me boughs off many a tree:
But thou wast up by break of day
And brought'st thy sweets along with thee . . .[1]

Mary Magdalene, too, was up at break of day: of all Jesus's
women disciples she was the most dear to him. In the agony of
Good Friday she had kept faith, standing close to the Cross;
through the dumb stillness of fear on Holy Saturday she had
mourned; then what a transcendent Sunday dawn this must
have been for her.

Other women among the disciples had been with her, but St
John tells that when they had gone she could not tear herself
away:

Mary stood without at the sepulchre weeping . . . and
saw Jesus standing, and knew that it was Jesus.

Jesus saith unto her, Woman, why weepest thou?
whom seekest thou? She, supposing him to be the
gardener, saith unto him, Sir, if thou have borne him
hence, tell me where thou hast laid him, and I will
take him away.

Jesus saith unto her, Mary. She turned herself, and
saith unto him, Rabboni; which is to say, Master.[2]

Easter Sunday, for Christians, is the most momentous day of the year.

> Can there be any day but this,
> Though many sunnes to shine endeavour?
> We count three hundred but we misse:
> There is but one, and that one ever.[3]

It is more important even than Christmas, which is only the beginning of the faith; Easter is its fulfilment.

It was necessary in God's plan that Christ, his only son, had to die; Jesus gives us the reason: 'I tell you . . . unless a wheat grain falls on the ground and dies, it remains only a single grain; but if it dies, it yields a rich harvest.'[4]

We are Christ's harvest all over the world, and if we follow him, he shows us clearly how to reap our own. It may be, too, that his suffering and ignominy were to help us keep our own sufferings in proportion; as he told us: 'I am the way, the truth and the life.' Easter is now, fresh life – eternal.

The apostles at first were afraid to believe in his rising, though they were shown it at first hand, as it were, by Christ himself; we have it only from the Gospels and they differ, so that it is no wonder that we doubt. We should be grateful, then, to St Thomas the Apostle, who had been absent when Christ first appeared: 'Except I shall . . . put my finger into the print of the nails, and thrust my hand into his side, I will not believe.' Then, though the doors were shut, Jesus appeared and said to Thomas, 'Reach hither thy finger . . . reach hither thy hand . . .' Thomas, overcome with awe, cried, 'My Lord and my God,' and Jesus gave the wonderful reply that has heartened us down the ages, 'Thomas, because thou hast seen me, thou hast believed: blessed are they that have not seen, and yet have believed.'[5]

Note

Mary Magdalene is one of the most famous women of all time; next to St Peter, she is the most vivid of the saints who were with Christ in his lifetime. For generations she was identified as Mary, sister of Martha in Bethany and their brother Lazarus, whom Christ had raised from the dead, or as the sinful Mary who, at Simon the Pharisee's supper, brought a box of precious ointment to anoint Jesus and washed his feet with her tears and wiped them with her hair, but now it is sure that she is quite another Mary, who came from Magdalene by the Sea of Galilee.

We do not know how she met Jesus, except that the Gospels say she was 'possessed by seven devils' (seven must have been strong and persistent, they may have been fits of madness or else of a way of life she could hardly resist). She may have been a courtesan at Herod's court, but Jesus, with infinite patience, healed her, and there grew between them a love that passes the world's understanding. She seems never to have left him again and, as we know, was the first to see him when he was risen.

Women ever since have been comforted and inspired by Mary Magdalene, especially those legions of us who have, as they used to say, 'fallen'. Jesus could have said of her, as he said of that other Mary of the precious ointment:

'Wheresoever this gospel shall be preached throughout the whole world, this also that she hath done shall be spoken of for a memorial of her.'[6]

1 From 'Easter' by George Herbert.

2 John 20:111, 14–16 (King James Bible).

3 From 'Easter' by George Herbert.

4 John 12:24 (Jerusalem Bible).

5 John 20:25, 27–9 (King James Bible).

6 Mark 14:9 (King James Bible).

THE BAKERWOMAN

The bakerwoman
  in her humble lodge
received a grain of wheat from God.
For nine whole months
  the grain she stored.
Behold the handmaid of the Lord.
Make us the bread, Mary, Mary.
Make us the bread.
  We need to be fed.

The bakerwoman took
  the road which led
to Bethlehem, the house of bread.
To knead the bread she laboured
  through the night,
and brought it forth about midnight.
Bake us the bread, Mary, Mary.
Bake us the bread.
  We need to be fed.

She baked the bread for thirty years
by the fire of her love
  and the salt of her tears,
by the warmth of a heart
  so tender and bright,
and the bread was golden
  brown and white.

Bring us the bread, Mary, Mary.
Bring us the bread.
  We need to be fed.

After thirty years
  the bread was done.
It was taken to town
  by her own son;
the soft white bread to be given free
to the hungry people of Galilee.
Give us the bread, Mary, Mary.
Give us the bread.
  We need to be fed.

For thirty coins the bread was sold,
and a thousand teeth so cold,
  so cold
tore it to pieces on a Friday noon
  and red the moon.
Break us the bread, Mary, Mary.
Break us the bread.
  We need to be fed.

And when she saw
  the bread so white,
the living bread she had made
  at night,
devoured as wolves might
devour a sheep,
the bakerwoman began to weep.

Weep for the bread, Mary, Mary.
Weep for the bread.
   We need to be fed.

But the bakerwoman's only son
appeared to his friends
   when three days had run
on the road which to Emmaus led,
and they knew him in
   the breaking of bread.
Lift up your head, Mary, Mary.
Lift up your head.
   For now we've been fed.

Herbert Richards

$\mathscr{T}$HE $\mathscr{D}$ONKEY

When fishes flew and forests walked
   And figs grew upon thorn,
Some moment when the moon was blood
   Then surely I was born.

With monstrous head and sickening cry
   and ears like errant wings,
The devil's walking parody
   On all four-footed things.

The tattered outlaw of the earth,
   Of ancient crooked will;
Starve, scourge, deride me: I am dumb,
   I keep my secret still.

Fools! For I also had my hour;
   One far fierce hour and sweet:
There was a shout about my ears,
   and palms before my feet.

G. K. Chesterton

From The Dream of the Rood

'I WAS RAISED UP A ROOD':
A TREE THAT BECAME A CROSS

Many years ago – the memory abides –
I was felled to the ground at the forest's edge,
Severed from my roots. Enemies seized me,
Made of me a mark of scorn for criminals to
    mount on . . .
I was raised up a Rood, a royal King I bore,
The High King of Heaven: hold firm I must.
They drove dark nails through me, the dire
    wounds still show,
Cruel gaping gashes, yet I dared not give as
    good.
They taunted the two of us; I was wet with
    teeming blood,
Streaming from the warrior's side when he
    sent forth his spirit.
High upon that hill helpless I suffered
Long hours of torment; I saw the Lord of
    Hosts
Outstretched in agony; all-embracing darkness
Covered with thick clouds the corpse of the
    World's Ruler;
The bright day was darkened by a deep
    shadow,

All its colours clouded; the whole creation
    wept,
Keened for its King's fall; Christ was on the
    Rood.

Anon.

From The Crosse

Who can blot out the Crosse, which
    th'instrument
Of God, dew'd on mee in the Sacrament?
Who can deny mee power, and liberty
To stretch mine armes, and mine owne Cross
    to be?
Swimme, and at every stroake, thou art thy
    Crosse;
The Mast and yard make one, where seas do
    tosse;
Looke downe, thou spiest out Crosses in small
    things;
Looke up, thou seest birds rais'd on crossed
    wings;
All the Globes frame, and spheares, is nothing
    else
But the Meridians crossing Parallels.
Materiall Crosses then, good physicke bee,
But yet spirituall have chiefe dignity.
These for extracted chimique medicine serve,
And cure much better, and as well preserve;
Then are you your own physicke, or need none,
When Still'd, or purg'd by tribulation.
For when that Cross ungrudg'd unto you
    stickes,
Then are you to your selfe, a Crucifixe.

As perchance, Carvers do not faces make,
But that away, which hid them there, do take;
Let Crosses, soe, take what hid Christ in thee,
And be his image, or not his, but hee.

John Donne

From I Did Not See it Then

NOW IN THE PLACE WHERE HE WAS
CRUCIFIED THERE WAS A GARDEN
(JOHN 19:41)

I did not see it then: that awful darkness
Was on us like His shroud:
I only heard the weeping of His mother,
The surging of the crowd.

Saw only, on the hill, a darker Shadow,
Outlined against the sky.
'Place of a skull' they called it, and I heard
   them,
Heard them, and watched Him die.

And when the night came, and it was all over,
They gave us down our Dead.
Joseph had begged it: and he brought fair
   linen
To wrap about His head.

And told us of a sepulchre new-finished,
Hewn in the rock near by,
It was his own; and thither then we bore Him,
The Sabbath drawing nigh.

Yet even then I thought not of the garden,
Black was the night and stark.
So Joseph held the lantern and we followed,
Bearing Him through the dark.

And suddenly the light flashed upon tree
    trunks,
Leaves that were silver-grey.
So had their torches flashed upon the olives.
God – was it yesterday?

Last night, beneath the glimmer of the olives,
They took Him, and we fled.
Tonight, beneath the glimmer of the olives,
We bore our Master, dead.

Yet even then I saw not, till the breaking
Of that eternal dawn,
When I came back and found the sunlight
    steeping
The dew upon the lawn.

Empty the tomb, and round it white-robed
    angels
Under the sky and far,
The glitter of the sunrise on the olives,
The paling of a star.

And upon Calvary's sharp-smitten summit,
Clear shining after rain,
Stood there the Cross, transfigured in that
   splendour
Its passion and its pain.

Helen Waddell

From Easter

I got me flowers to straw thy way;
I got me boughs off many a tree:
But thou wast up by break of day,
And brought'st thy sweets along with thee.

The Sunne arising in the East,
Though he give light, & th'East perfume;
If they should offer to contest
With thy arising, they presume.

Can there be any day but this,
Though many sunnes to shine endeavour?
We count three hundred, but we misse:
There is but one, and that one ever.

George Herbert

CREATION

To revel in the wonders of Creation without giving a thought to the One who made it is like loving someone's poems and ignoring the poet.

> The world is charged with the grandeur of
> God.
>> It will flame out, like shining from shook
>> foil;
>> It gathers to a greatness, like the ooze of
>> oil
> Crushed. Why do men then now not reck his
> rod?
> Generations have trod, have trod, have trod;
>> And all is seared with trade; bleared,
>> smeared with toil;
>> And wears man's smudge and shares man's
>> smell: the soil
> Is bare now, nor can foot feel, being shod.
>
> And for all this, nature is never spent;
>> There lives the dearest freshness deep down
>> things;
> And though the last lights off the black West
> went

Oh, morning, at the brown brink eastward,
    springs –
Because the Holy Ghost over the bent
    World broods with warm breast and with
      ah! bright wings.[1]

1 'God's Grandeur' by GERARD MANLEY HOPKINS.

This is the time of year when, even for the
old,
Youngness comes knocking on the heart
undefined
Aches and announcements – blurred felicities
foretold,
And (obvious utterance) wearying winter left
behind.

I never felt it more than now, when out
beyond these safening walls
Sculptured with Stations of the Cross, spring-
confident, unburdened, bold,
The first March blackbird overhead to forward
vision flutes and calls.
You could have said this simple thing, old self,
in any previous year.
But not to that one ritual flame – to that all-
answering Heart abidant here.

Siegfried Sassoon

Here the trees of the Lord are full of sap; the
cedars of Lebanon, which he hath planted;
Where the birds make their nests: as for the
stork, the fir trees are her house.
The high hills are a refuge for the wild goats;
and the rocks for the conies.
He appointed the moon for seasons: the sun
knoweth his going down.
Thou makest darkness, and it is night: wherein
all the beasts of the forest do creep forth.
The young lions roar after their prey, and
seek their meat from God.
The sun ariseth, they gather themselves
together, and lay them down in their dens.
Man goeth forth unto his work and to his
labour until the evening.
O LORD, how manifold are thy works! in
wisdom hast thou made them all: the earth
is full of thy riches.
So is this great and wide sea, wherein are
things creeping innumerable, both small and
great beasts.
There go the ships: there is that leviathan,
whom thou hast made to play therein.
These wait all upon thee; that thou mayest
give them their meat in due season.

That thou givest them they gather: thou
  openest thine hand, they are filled with
  good.
Thou hidest thy face, they are troubled: thou
  takest away their breath, they die, and
  return to their dust.
Thou sendest forth thy spirit, they are created:
  and thou renewest the face of the earth.
The glory of the LORD shall endure for ever:
  the LORD shall rejoice in his works.

(King James Bible)

The Tyger

Tyger! Tyger! burning bright
In the forests of the night,
What immortal hand or eye
Could frame thy fearful symmetry?

In what distant deeps or skies
Burnt the fire of thine eyes?
On what wings dare he aspire?
What the hand dare seize the fire?

And what shoulder, & what art,
Could twist the sinews of thy heart?
And when thy heart began to beat,
What dread hand? & what dread feet?

What the hammer? what the chain?
In what furnace was thy brain?
What the anvil? what dread grasp
Dare its deadly terrors clasp?

When the stars threw down their spears,
And water'd heaven with their tears,
Did he smile his work to see?
Did he who made the Lamb make thee?

Tyger! Tyger! burning bright
In the forests of the night,
What immortal hand or eye,
Dare frame thy fearful symmetry?

William Blake

FROM INSCRIPTION ON THE MONUMENT OF A NEWFOUNDLAND DOG (EXTRACT)

When some proud son of man returns to
    earth,
Unknown to glory, but upheld by birth,
The sculptor's art exhausts the pomp of
    woe,
And storied urns record who rests below;

But the poor dog, in life the firmest
    friend,
The first to welcome, foremost to defend,
Whose honest heart is still his master's
    own,
Who labours, fights, lives, breathes for him
    alone,
Unhonour'd falls, unnoticed all his worth,
Denied in heaven the soul he held on
    earth.

While man, vain insect! hopes to be
    forgiven,
And claims himself a sole exclusive heaven.
Each kindred brute might bid thee blush for
    shame.

Ye! who perchance behold this simple urn,
Pass on – it honours none you wish to mourn:
To mark a friend's remains these stones arise;
I never knew but one, – and here he lies.

George Gordon, Lord Byron

$\mathscr{T}$HE $\mathscr{R}$ED $\mathscr{C}$OCKATOO

Sent as a present from Annam –
A red cockatoo.
Coloured like the peach-tree blossom,
Speaking with the speech of men.

And they did to it what is always done
To the learned and eloquent.
They took a cage with stout bars
And shut it up inside.

Po Chū-i (tr. Arthur Waley)

LITTLE THINGS THAT RUN AND QUAIL

Little things that run and quail
And die in silence and despair;

Little things that fight and fail
And fall on earth and sea and air;

All trapped and frightened little things
The mouse, the coney, hear our prayer.

As we forgive those done to us,
The lamb, the linnet, and the hare,

Forgive us all our trespasses,
Little creatures everywhere.

James Stephens

FLOWER IN THE CRANNIED WALL

Flower in the crannied wall,
I pluck you out of the crannies,
I hold you here, root and all, in my hand,
Little flower – but *if* I could understand
What you are, root and all, and all in all,
I should know what God and man is.

Alfred, Lord Tennyson

$\mathcal{E}$XILE

Then, I had no doubt
That snowdrops, violets, all creatures, I myself
Were lovely, were loved, were love.
Look, they said,
And I had only to look deep into the heart,
Dark, deep into the violet, and there read,
Before I knew of any word for flower or love,
The flower, the love, the word.

They never wearied of telling their being; and I
Asked of the rose, only more rose, the violet
More violet; untouched by time
No flower withered or flame died,
But poised in its own eternity, until the looker
   moved
On to another flower, opening its entity.

Kathleen Raine

FROM LATIN LYRICS

Take thou this rose, O Rose,
Since Love's own flower it is,
And by that rose
  Thy lover captive is.

Smell thou this rose, O Rose,
And know thyself as sweet
  As dawn is sweet.

Look on this rose, O Rose,
And looking, laugh on me,
And in thy laughter's ring
  The nightingale shall sing . . .

O Rose, this painted rose
Is not the whole;
Who paints the flower
  Paints not its fragrant soul.

Anon. (tr. Helen Waddell)

FROM IMMANENCE

I come in the little things,
Saith the Lord:
Not borne on morning wings
Of majesty, but I have set My Feet
Amidst the delicate and bladed wheat
That springs triumphant in the furrowed sod.

There do I dwell, in weakness and in
    power;
Not broken or divided, saith our God!
In your strait garden plot I come to flower:
About your porch My Vine
Meek, fruitful, doth entwine;
Waits, at the threshold, Love's appointed
    hour ...

I come in the little things,
Saith the Lord:
My starry wings
I do forsake,
Love's highway of humility to take:
Meekly I fit My Stature to your need.
In beggar's part
About your gates I shall not cease to
    plead —

As man, to speak with man –
Till by such art
I shall achieve My Immemorial Plan,
Pass the low lintel of the human heart.

Evelyn Underhill

${\mathcal{S}}$PIRIT: PENTECOST

$\mathcal{P}$entecost is the day when, after Christ has ascended to
heaven leaving a chosen twelve of his disciples,
cowering in a hidden room, they were made apostles:

> . . . they had all met in one room, when suddenly they
> heard what sounded like a powerful wind from heaven,
> the noise of which filled the entire house in which they
> were sitting; and something appeared to them that
> seemed like tongues of fire; these separated and came
> to rest on the head of each of them. They were all filled
> with the Holy Spirit, and began to speak foreign
> languages as the Spirit gave them the gift of speech.
>
> Now there were devout men living in Jerusalem
> from every nation under heaven, and at this sound
> they all assembled, each one bewildered to hear these
> men speaking his own language. They were amazed
> and astonished. 'Surely,' they said, 'all these men
> speaking are Galileans? How does it happen that
> . . . we hear them preaching in our own language
> about the marvels of God?' Everyone was amazed and
> unable to explain it; they asked one another what it all
> meant. Some, however, laughed it off. 'They have
> been drinking too much new wine,' they said.[1]

A disciple is a follower who can listen and believe quietly, but an apostle is a witness, a messenger who must speak, teach, lead and inspire: 'Peter stood up with the Eleven and addressed them in a loud voice: "Men of Judaea, and all you who live in Jerusalem, make no mistake about this, but listen carefully to what I say. These men are not drunk, as you imagine; why, it is only the third hour of the day . . ." '[2]

Peter had been an ordinary fisherman – it is probable he could neither read nor write. In his three years of following Jesus he was brash, impetuous, often, through sheer ignorance, misunderstanding, yet Jesus chose him to be his Church's first leader – and wisely; the name Peter means 'rock', and Christ had said to this unlikely man, 'Thou art Peter, and upon this rock I will build my church.' On that very first day, Peter was able to speak to the crowd with what could not have been more telling eloquence as he interpreted his Master's will:

> In the days to come – it is the Lord who
> speaks –
> I will pour out my spirit on all mankind.
> Their sons and daughters shall prophesy,
> your young men shall see visions,
> your old men shall dream dreams;
> Even on my slaves, men and women,
> in those days, I will pour out my spirit.[3]

We are apt to believe that our spirit belongs to us, whereas, in reality, we belong to it, are animated, prompted – sometimes adversely or, on the contrary, marvellously –

by it. It is always original and not dependent on genes – another popular belief. Parents are puzzled when their children manifest a spirit quite different – sometimes startlingly different – from their own: 'Where did he or she get it from?' they wonder.

Our minds are led by the spirit: isn't it the spirit that upholds the work, the endless patient research, of scientists, doctors, engineers and artists? Painters, composers, writers are perhaps closest to the marvel of creation, with a spirit that is usually unquenchable: a young man born without hands has become a considerable painter, needing no concessions because of his disability. His *Winter Landscape*, made into a Christmas card, has become known nationwide – but how could he paint it? He painted it with his mouth. In everyday life the spirit can be equally potent; for instance, a woman widowed or deserted with three children, and hardly any money, who manages to bring them up decently and, more important, happily probably has a stronger and more enduring spirit than the first astronaut to walk on the moon.

Some of us, refusing to believe in 'spirit' call it a 'life force'; well, life certainly is forceful, and not only in people; we see it in animals - even in plants. Flowers in a room can, if you are sensitive, send you a message, a sudden waft of scent to remind you of their presence. A scilla, that little blue spring bulb, was once, by mistake, planted upside-down in the autumn; its hidden struggle must have gone on all winter, but in the spring it was found flowering into the earth, perfect except that its normal deep blue was pale. The most phenomenal thing about the spirit is that the more one draws on it, the stronger it grows.

Yet take heed, Peter warns us, 'until the day dawn, and the day star arise in your hearts,'[4] and indeed we have to be on our guard: modern churches do not like to use the condemnation of the word 'sin', but they, and we, cannot deny that sinful – evil – spirits are rampant. The New Testament testifies to this over and over again, and we have only to read the newspapers or watch television to be forced to admit how powerful, and persuasive, they are. The Governor of the Maison Centrale prison in France, where only the worst criminals go, was the most humane and helpful of prison governors, yet she said, 'I don't know if I believe in God, but I do believe in the devil. I have met him.'

One needs courage to fight him – but the gift that came to the apostles that day of Pentecost was not only a powerful wind but a fire. Peter had been a coward; on the night Jesus was arrested in the garden, Peter denied three times that he had ever known him, yet in his mission he faced beatings, imprisonment, exile without flinching and finally followed his Master to crucifixion, a death even more ignominious because he was nailed to his cross head down.

He did not leave his Church without a guide; while he lived he wrote, or dictated, letters that, from the New Testament, still seem to speak directly to us.

1 Acts 2: 1–13 (Jerusalem Bible).

2 ibid, 3: 11–13 (Jerusalem Bible).

3 ibid, 2: 17 (Jerusalem Bible).

4 2 Peter 1:19 (King James Bible).

From The Upanishads

THE HOLY SPIRIT, AS SHOWN IN CREATION
AND HUMAN KIND, RUNS ALL THROUGH
THIS LITTLE BOOK AS IT HAS ALWAYS
DONE IN LIFE AND IN TRUE POETRY

In this body, in this town of Spirit, there is a little house shaped like a lotus and in that house there is a little space . . . There is as much in that little space within the heart as there is in the whole world outside. Heaven, earth, fire, wind, sun, moon, lightning, stars; whatever is and whatever is not, everything is there . . . What lies in that space does not decay when the body decays, nor does it fall when the body falls. That space is the home of Spirit. Every desire is there. Self is there, beyond decay and death; sin and sorrow; hunger and thirst; His aim truth; His will truth.

THE CAGED SKYLARK

As a dare-gale skylark scanted in a dull cage
    Man's mounting spirit in his bone-house,
        mean house, dwells –
    That bird beyond the remembering his free
        fells,
This is in drudgery, day-labouring-out life's
    age.

Though aloft on turf or perch or poor low
    stage,
    Both sing sometimes the sweetest, sweetest
        spells,
    Yet both droop deadly sometimes in their
        cells
Or wring their barriers in bursts of fear or
    rage.

Not that the sweet-fowl, song-fowl, needs no
    rest –
Why, hear him, hear him babble and drop
    down to his nest.
    But his own nest, wild nest, no prison.

Man's spirit will be flesh-bound when found at
　　best,
But uncumberèd: meadow-down is not
　　distressed
　　For a rainbow footing it nor he for his
　　　　bones risen.

Gerard Manley Hopkins

The Kingdom of God

O world invisible, we view thee,
O world intangible, we touch thee,
O world unknowable, we know thee,
Inapprehensible, we clutch thee!

Does the fish soar to find the ocean,
The eagle plunge to find the air –
That we ask of the stars in motion
If they have rumour of thee there?

Not where the wheeling systems darken,
And our benumb'd conceiving soars! –
The drift of pinions, would we hearken,
Beats at our own clay-shuttered doors.

The angels keep their ancient places; –
Turn but a stone, and start a wing!
'Tis ye, 'tis your estrangèd faces,
That miss the many-splendoured thing.

But (when so sad thou canst not sadder)
Cry; – and upon thy so sore loss
Shall shine the traffic of Jacob's ladder
Pitched betwixt Heaven and Charing Cross.

Yea, in the night, my Soul, my daughter,
Cry – clinging Heaven by the hems;
And lo, Christ walking on the water
Not of Gennesareth but Thames!

Francis Thompson

$\mathcal{F}$OLLOW $\mathcal{M}$E

A BUDDHIST POEM

He who is Blessing passed by my hut,
passed me, the barber.*
I ran and he turned, waited
for me, the barber!
I said, 'May I speak to you, Lord?'
He said, 'Yes.'
   'Yes', to *me*, the barber!
I said, 'Can your Peace be for a person like
   me?'
He said, 'Yes.'
His Peace for *me*, the barber!
I said, 'May I follow you, Lord?'
He said, 'Yes,'
to *me*, the barber!
I said, 'May I stay close to you, Lord?'
He said, 'You may,'
close to *me*, the poor barber!

Anon.

*In Hindu India a barber is an 'untouchable'.

FROM ULYSSES

There lies the port; the vessel puffs her sail:
There gloom the dark broad seas. My
   mariners,
Souls that have toil'd, and wrought, and
   thought with me . . .
you and I are old;
Old age hath yet his honour and his toil;
Death closes all: but something ere the end,
Some work of noble note, may yet be done,
Not unbecoming men that strove with gods.
The lights begin to twinkle from the rocks:
The long day wanes: the slow moon climbs:
   the deep
Moans round with many voices. Come, my
   friends,
'Tis not too late to seek a newer world . . .
for my purpose holds
To sail beyond the sunset, and the baths
Of all the western stars, until I die.
It may be that the gulfs will wash us down:
It may be we shall touch the Happy Isles.

                        Alfred, Lord Tennyson

$\mathcal{H}$AIKU

Live in simple faith . . .
   just as this
   trusting cherry
flowers, fades, and falls.

Issa

I went to the dances at Chandlerville,
And played snap-out at Winchester.
One time we changed partners,
Driving home in the moonlight of middle
    June,
And then I found Davis.
We were married and lived together for
    seventy years,
Enjoying, working, raising the twelve
    children,
Eight of whom we lost
Ere I had reached the age of sixty.
I spun, I wove, I kept the house, I nursed the
    sick,
I made the garden, and for holiday
Rambled over the fields where sang the
    larks,
And by Spoon River gathering many a shell,
And many a flower and medicinal weed –
Shouting to the wooded hills, singing to the
    green valleys.
At ninety-six I had lived enough, that is
    all,
And passed to a sweet repose.
What is this I hear of sorrow and weariness,
Anger, discontent and drooping hopes?

Degenerate sons and daughters,
Life is too strong for you –
It takes life to love Life.

Edgar Lee Masters

LEGEND

The blacksmith's boy went out with a rifle
and a black dog running behind.
Cobwebs snatched at his feet,
rivers hindered him,
thorn-branches caught at his eyes to make him
   blind
and the sky turned into an unlucky opal,
but he didn't mind.
I can break branches, I can swim rivers, I can
   stare out any spider I meet,
said he to his dog and his rifle.

The blacksmith's boy went over the paddocks
with his old black hat on his head.
Mountains jumped in his way,
rocks rolled down on him,
and the old crow cried, You'll soon be dead;
and the rain came down like mattocks.
But he only said
I can climb mountains, I can dodge rocks, I
   can shoot an old crow any day.
And he went on over the paddocks.

When he came to the end of the day the sun
    began falling.
Up came the night ready to swallow him,
like the barrel of a gun,
like an old black hat,
like a black dog hungry to follow him.
Then the pigeon, the magpie and the dove
    began wailing,
and the grass lay down to pillow him.
His rifle broke, his hat blew away and his dog
    was gone,
and the sun was falling.

But in front of the night the rainbow stood on
    the mountain
just as his heart foretold.
He ran like a hare,
he climbed like a fox,
he caught it in his hands, the colours and the
    cold –
like a bar of ice, like the column of a fountain,
like a ring of gold.
The pigeon, the magpie and the dove flew up
    to stare,
and the grass stood up again on the mountain.

The blacksmith's boy hung the rainbow on his
    shoulder
instead of his broken gun.
Lizards ran out to see,
snakes made way for him,
and the rainbow shone as brightly as the sun.
All the world said, Nobody is braver, nobody
    is bolder,
nobody else has done
anything to equal it. He went home as easy as
    could be
with the swinging rainbow on his shoulder.

Judith Wright

Things Men Have Made

Things men have made with wakened hands,
    and put soft life into
are awake through years with transferred
    touch, and go on glowing
for long years.
And for this reason, some old things are lovely,
warm still with the life of forgotten men who
    made them.

D. H. Lawrence

Whatever Man Makes

Whatever man makes and makes it live
lives because of the life put into it.
A yard of India muslin is alive with Hindu life.
And a Navajo woman, weaving her rug in the
    pattern of her dream,
must run the pattern out in a little break at
    the end
so that her soul can come out back to her.
But in the odd pattern, like snake-marks on
    the sand, it leaves its trail.

D. H. Lawrence

O<small>N</small> H<small>IS</small> B<small>LINDNESS</small>

When I consider how my light is spent,
   E're half my days, in this dark world and wide,
   And that one Talent which is death to hide,
   Lodg'd with me useless, though my Soul
      more bent
To serve therewith my Maker, and present
   My true account, lest he returning chide,
   Doth God exact day-labour, light denied,
   I fondly ask; but Patience, to prevent
That murmur, soon replies: God doth not need
   Either man's work or his own gifts; who best
   Bear his milde yoke, they serve him best.
      His State
Is Kingly. Thousands at his bidding speed
   And post o'er Land and Ocean without rest;
   They also serve who only stand and wait.

John Milton

Give me my scallop-shell of quiet,
My staff of faith to walk upon,
My scrip of joy, immortal diet,
My bottle of salvation,
My gown of glory, hope's true gage;
And thus I'll take my pilgrimage.

Blood must be my body's balmer;
No other balm will there be given;
Whilst my soul like a white palmer
Travels to the land of heaven;
Over the silver mountains,
Where spring the nectar fountains:
    There will I kiss
    The bowl of bliss;
And drink mine everlasting fill
On every milken hill.
My soul will be a-dry before,
But after, it will thirst no more ...

Sir Walter Raleigh

ALL SAINTS, ALL SOULS

*T*he eve of All Saints, or All Hallows, falls on the last day of October, the 31st, which in our old Celtic calendar – before Christianity came to the West – was the night given over to black magic, when wizards and witches, and ghosts who could not rest because of their sins, roamed, disturbing everyone with their power. The hierarchy of the early Church deliberately placed their own feast of All Saints/Hallows on the day after this evil eve, thinking that the saints' holy power would wipe out these ancient superstitions; but they discounted the attraction of Hallowe'en, as it came to be called, an attraction particularly for children who, by tradition, are given licence, as soon as it is dusk, to tease grown-ups and 'flirt', as it were, with being bad.

It is not meant to go very far; the great tease is 'Trick or Treat', when children, dressed up as ghosts – usually in white sheets – witches, black cats, owls or bats, have the right to knock at front doors and, when they are opened, to demand, 'Trick or Treat?' Wise grown-ups are ready for the 'Treat', providing themselves with toffee apples, sweets, oranges and nuts, and they have the right to say: 'First ask me a riddle or sing me a song,' but if they are rash enough to say, 'Trick,' or start to shut the door, a burst bag of flour may be thrown at them, making a magnificent mess.

Sometimes the teasing – or tormenting – goes too far, with older boys and girls carried away by the excitement doing real damage; in homes where a fire is lit they may climb silently up a ladder to put a turf on the chimney, so that choking smoke fills the whole house; they may let pigs out into a garden or on to a road, or cover the windows and windscreens of cars with paint.

For younger children, too, there is often an undercurrent of fear from the Hallowe'en tales of witches, ghosts and children being kidnapped by will-o'-the wisp magic, like the haunting tale of Hazel Dorn:

> . . . Swiftly her arms they bound in gossamer,
> With elvish lures they held her soul in thrall;
> With wizard sorceries enveloped her
>   Past cry or call.
>
> A passing shepherd caught his breath to see
> A golden mist of moving wings and lights
> Swirl upwards past the red moon eerily
>   To starlit heights.
>
> While far-off carollings half drowned a cry,
> Mournful, remote, of 'Mother, Mother dear,'
> Floating across the drifting haze – a sight
>   'Farewell, Farewell'[1]

That is horridly haunting for a child to go to sleep on, but in the morning comes the benign comfort of All Saints.

No exorciser harm thee!
Nor no witchcraft charm thee!
Ghost unlaid forbear thee!
Nothing ill comes near thee!
Quiet consummation have:
And renowned be thy grave![2]

In the Christian faith, saints are invoked to help us. The greatest saint of all is the quiet St Joseph; closest to Christ in his carpenter's shop, he is Joseph the Workman, who can help us in our daily work; he is also the saint to call upon when we are dying. Most of us know that St Anthony is the one who finds things when they are lost; St Blaize will cure sore throats; St Jude is often forgotten but is most important because he is the saint of lost causes, when all hope has gone; while St Christopher is the one for travellers – countless cars have a small medallion of St Christopher fastened to the dashboard, and it was he who is supposed to have whispered in a speed hog's ear, as his speedometer went over 100 mph, 'Now you are on your own.'

The saints are, too, for comfort and strength in sorrow, and the Church, again deliberately, made the contingent day, 2 November, the 'solemnity' of All Souls, remembrance of the dead. The remembrance goes on all through the month; in some churches lists of loved names are brought to be put on the altar. November is thought of as bleak and chill, but All Souls is not a gloomy festival; of course there is sadness – we miss people so much – yet it is a joyful feast because this 'remembering' means our dead are still very much with us.

They always are. Spiritualists, in their earnestness, claim they can put us in touch with those who have died – but they are interfering with they know not what; it seems better to accept the natural way. Don't the dead come to mind on birthdays and anniversaries and, especially, in our daily life as, in our homes, we touch and use ordinary things? 'Grandfather left me those lamps'; 'Mother gave me these little silver coffee spoons'; 'The old gardener, Mr McAllister, planted these roses – I wish he could see them now' (perhaps he can). And not only things: 'How Deborah loved that book' . . . 'James that music.' We don't need photographs to see the people we have loved.

> There is time of weeping and there is time of laughing. But as you see, he setteth the weeping time before, for that is the time of this wretched world and the laughing time shall come after in heaven. There is also a time of sowing, and a time of reaping too. Now must we in this world sow, that we may in the other world reap: and in this short sowing time of this weeping world, must we water our seed with the showers of our tears, and then shall we have in heaven a merry laughing harvest for ever.[3]

1 Bernard Sleigh.

2 William Shakespeare: *Cymbeline*, Act IV, sc. ii.

3 Sir Thomas More,

One Foot in Eden

One foot in Eden still, I stand
And look across the other land.
The world's great day is growing late,
Yet strange these fields that we have planted
So long with crops of love and hate.
Time's handiworks by time are haunted,
And nothing now can separate
The corn and tares compactly grown.
The armorial weed in stillness bound
About the stalk; these are our own.
Evil and good stand thick around
In the fields of charity and sin
Where we shall lead our harvest in.

Yet still from Eden springs the root
As clean as on the starting day.
Time takes the foliage and the fruit
And burns the archetypal leaf
To shapes of terror and of grief
Scattered along the winter way.
But famished field and blackened tree
Bear flowers in Eden never known.
Blossoms of grief and charity
Bloom in these darkened fields alone.
What had Eden ever to say
Of hope and faith and pity and love

Until was buried all its day
And memory found its treasure trove?
Strange blessings never in Paradise
Fall from these beclouded skies.

Edwin Muir

From Fare Well

Look thy last on all things lovely,
Every hour – let no night
Seal thy sense in deathly slumber
   Till to delight
Thou hast paid thy utmost blessing;
Since that all things thou wouldst praise
Beauty took from those who loved them
   In other days.

Walter de la Mare

WHEN EARTH'S LAST PICTURE IS PAINTED

When Earth's last picture is painted and the
    tubes are twisted and dried,
When the oldest colours have faded, and the
    youngest critic has died,
We shall rest, and, faith, we shall need it – lie
    down for an aeon or two,
Till the Master of All Good Workmen shall
    put us to work anew.

And those that were good shall be happy: they
    shall sit in a golden chair;
They shall splash at a ten-league canvas with
    brushes of comets' hair.
They shall find real saints to draw from –
    Magdalene, Peter, and Paul;
They shall work for an age at a sitting and
    never be tired at all!

And only The Master shall praise us, and only
  The Master shall blame;
And no one shall work for money, and no one
  shall work for fame,
But each for the joy of the working, and each,
  in his separate star,
Shall draw the Thing as he sees it for the
  God of Things as they are!

Rudyard Kipling

The Chinese Methuselah

Peng lived to a great age,
Yet he went at last, when he longed to stay.
And late or soon, all go:
Wise and simple have no reprieve.
Wine may bring forgetfulness,
But does it not hasten old age?
If you set your heart on noble deeds,
How do you know that any will praise you?
By all this thinking you do Me injury:
You had better go where Fate leads –
Drift on the Stream of Infinite Flux,
Without joy, without fear;
When you must go – then go,
And make as little fuss as you can.

Tao Ch'sen (tr. by Arthur Waley)

EPITAPH

Here lies, but seven years old, our little maid:
Once of the darkness – oh! so sore afraid.
Light of the World – remember that small
    fear,
And when nor moon nor stars do shine – draw
    near!

Walter de la Mare

From No Coward Soul is Mine

THE FOLLOWING ARE THE LAST LINES MY
SISTER EMILY EVER WROTE (NOTE BY
CHARLOTTE BRONTË)

No coward soul is mine,
No trembler in the world's storm-troubled
  sphere:
I see Heaven's glories shine,
And Faith shines equal, arming me from Fear.

Oh God within my breast,
Almighty, ever present Deity!
Life, that in me has rest,
As I, undying Life, have power in Thee!

Though earth and moon were gone,
And suns and universes ceased to be,
And Thou wert left alone,
Every existence would exist in Thee.

There is not room for Death,
Nor atom that his might could render void:
Thou – Thou art Being and Breath,
And what Thou art may never be destroyed.

Emily Brontë

Fear no more the heat o' the sun,
Nor the furious winter's rages;
Thou thy worldly task hast done,
Home art gone, and ta'en thy wages;
Golden lads and girls all must,
As chimney-sweepers, come to dust.

Fear no more the frown o' the great,
Thou art past the tyrant's stroke;
Care no more to clothe and eat;
To thee the reed is as the oak:
The sceptre, learning, physic, must
All follow this, and come to dust.

Fear no more the lightning flash,
Nor the all-dreaded thunder-stone;
Fear not slander, censure rash;
Thou hast finish'd joy and moan:
All lovers young, all lovers must
Consign to thee, and come to dust.

No exorciser harm thee!
Nor no witchcraft charm thee!
Ghost unlaid forbear thee!

Nothing ill come near thee!
Quiet consummation have:
And renowned be thy grave!

William Shakespeare

THIS QUIET DUST WAS GENTLEMEN
AND LADIES

This quiet dust was gentlemen and ladies
And lads and girls –
Was laughter and ability and sighing
And frocks and curls.

This passive place a summer's nimble mansion
Where bloom and bees
Exist an oriental circuit
Then cease, like these –

Emily Dickinson

From That Nature is a Heraclitean Fire and of the Comfort of the Resurrection

Enough! the Resurrection,
A heart-clarion! Away grief's gasping, joyless
   days, dejection.
      Across my foundering deck shone
A beacon, an eternal beam. Flesh fade, and
   mortal trash
Fall to the residuary worm; world's wildfire,
   leave but ash:
      In a flash, at a trumpet crash,
I am all at once what Christ is, since he was
   what I am, and
This Jack, joke, poor potsherd,
   patch, matchwood, immortal diamond.
      Is immortal diamond.

Gerard Manley Hopkins

$\mathscr{P}$EACE

My soul, there is a country
   Far beyond the stars,
Where stands a wingèd sentry
   All skilful in the wars;
There, above noise and danger,
   Sweet Peace sits crown'd with smiles,
And One born in a manger
   Commands the beauteous files.
He is thy gracious Friend,
   And – O my soul, awake! –
Did in pure love descend
   To die here for thy sake.
If thou canst get but thither,
   There grows the flower of Peace,
The Rose that cannot wither,
   Thy fortress, and thy ease.
Leave then thy foolish ranges,
   For none can thee secure,
But one who never changes –
Thy God, thy life, thy cure.

Henry Vaughan

From Morte d' Arthur

The old order changeth, yielding place to new,
And God fulfils Himself in many ways,
Lest one good custom should corrupt the world.
Comfort thyself: what comfort is in me?
I have lived my life, and that which I have done
May He within Himself make pure! but thou,
If thou should'st never see my face again,
Pray for my soul. More things are wrought by
    prayer
Than this world dreams of. Wherefore let thy
    voice
Rise like a fountain for me night and day.
For what are men better than sheep or goats
That nourish a blind life within the brain,
If, knowing God, they lift not hands of prayer
Both for themselves and those who call them
    friend?
For so the whole round earth is every way
Bound by gold chains about the feet of God.

Alfred, Lord Tennyson

ℰNVOY

Go, little book, and wish to all
Flowers in the garden, meat in the hall,
    A bin of wine, a spice of wit,
A house with lawns enclosing it,
    A living river by the door,
A nightingale in the sycamore!

Robert Louis Stevenson

INDEX OF FIRST LINES

$\mathscr{A}$CKNOWLEDGMENTS

For permission to reprint copyright material the publishers are grateful to the following:

Louise de Bruin and Gerard Casey for 'Mary of Nazareth' from *Annunciation*, first published in *Christophoros*, The Enitharmon Press, 1981, reprinted in *The Clear Shadow*, Rigby & Lewis, 1992, copyright © Gerard Casey; Constable Publishers for 'The Red Cockatoo' by Po Chū-i and 'I Did Not See It Then' by Helen Waddell; Faber & Faber for 'One Foot in Eden' by Edwin Muir; HarperCollins for 'Exile' by Kathleen Raine; The Harvill Press for Roy Campbell: from *The Poems of St John of the Cross*, first published by The Harvill Press in 1951. All rights reserved. Reproduced by permission of The Harvill Press; David Higham Associates for 'Fern Hill' by Dylan Thomas, from *The Poems* published by J. M. Dent, and for 'Timothy Winters' by Charles Causley, from *Collected Poems* published by Macmillan; Macmillan for 'The Oxen' by Thomas Hardy, from *The Complete Poems* published by Papermac, and for 'I Came Out Alone on My Way to My Tryst' by Rabindranath Tagore, published by Macmillan General Books; Mollie Martin for 'Latin Lyrics' translated by Helen Waddell; Ellen and Hilary Masters for 'Lucinda Matlock' by Edgar Lee Masters, from *Spoon River Anthology*, originally published by Macmillan. Reproduced by permission of Ellen C. Masters; John Murray